AF266192

together
we
RISE

Poems
and Incantations
to Heal the Witch Wound
and Awaken the Goddess Within

KIMBERLEY JONES

H

Herstory Books

Thank You

For the women who have walked before me.

For those who walk behind.

For my sisters walking beside me today.

Special thanks to Katherine, Cath and Ziggy.

My mother gave birth to me twice.

On the day I left her body.

Then on the day she left hers.

Contents

Introduction

My poem 'Together We Rise' poured through me in 2021.
At Samhain that same year, I sat in circle with sisters, around a fire in the woods, and read it aloud. We spoke of the Witch Wound and the Burning Times and how women were starting to wake up to the dark legacy of those 300 years of fear.

For the last 20 years my work has been fuelled by my own fire to help women heal that Witch Wound and reclaim their power, remembering their inherent magic within.

I coined the term Witch Wound. I wrote a school play about it when I was a child. I grew up watching my Clairvoyant Medium mother hide her gifts behind closed doors. My father inflamed to rage by her knowing. I watched my grandmother suppress her gifts and wither to ash as a result. I saw the fear and judgement of others about things they did not understand.

The Witch Wound is a past life imprint, an ancestral wound and a collective trauma, a deep cellular memory carried down through generations and perpetuated in our patriarchal society today. I feel it deeply.

The Burning Times were about destroying what men in power feared most; the Sacred Feminine, anything connected to Her and the women who embodied Her. And now SHE is returning. This book celebrates that.

For more about my work visit my website www.kimberleyjones.com

Part One:

Out of the Flames

WOMEN

They weren't Witches.
They were Women.

Return of My Power

You had no choice,
You lost your voice.
Lives depended on it.

Women spurned,
Midwives burned.
A past life scar imprinted.

Sacred rage
now dissolve my cage
of safety, now constricting.

This is my hour,
return of my power,
magic and medicine shining.

THE FIRE IN YOU

Women burned.
Wounds learned.
A lineage of hiding.

It's time to heal,
and to reveal,
the fire in us residing.

A Hope

Their silence and hiding,
running from the flames,
refusing to give names,
is why we are here today.

The things they couldn't say,
the ways they couldn't be,
held a hope of future we.

Keeping treasures close,
locked away,
until one day
we rose.

Blazing

Her power
burns brighter
than any flame
that sought to destroy Her.

Return of Her Magic

Try as they might

they can't kill our light.

Goddess cannot be burned.

Again and again a soul takes flight.

The magic always returns.

In her body

I often wonder
how many illnesses
women struggle with
are ancestral,
internalised,
witch wounds.

Sisterhood Wound

My sisters turned on me
and turned me in.

Took from me.
Betrayed me.

To save themselves.
To gain themselves.

I rage.
I grieve.
I can barely believe,
what they did.

And then....

Clarity.
I see.
They were no more free
than me.

RECLAIMING

The shaming and blaming,
gaslighting, defaming.
Narcissistic reframing,
of truth.

She hasn't mattered.
Sacredness shattered.
An object, commodity.
No proof.

Except for depression,
the pain and suppression,
of mothers' and daughters',
lost youth.

Internalised pain,
now becoming our reign,
reclaiming our magic.
Forsooth.

Fire of Freedom

Your flames that sought to destroy me,

to destroy Her,

to destroy us,

burn ever brighter in our daughters.

Fire of freedom.

For a new Earth.

Dark Feminine

Deep diving

into the watery womb

of death and renewal.

Hecate dancing

with our wounds.

Sink.

Surrender.

Ready to rise

and breathe anew.

Know This

My body is mine.
My voice is mine.
My gifts are mine.
Know this.

You do not define me.
You cannot confine me.
I am free.
Know this.

I am Goddess.
I am nature.
I am eternal.
Know this.

Your time has ended.
My fire has ascended.
My time is now.
Know this.

Wise and Wild

From wounded maidens,

to wise and wild mothers,

enchantresses and crones.

We are now waking and walking with Her,

rooted in our bones.

Safe to be ME

It is now safe for me to
share my gifts
speak my truth
reveal my magic.
Be me.

My throat is healing,
voice revealing.
It's safe for me to be seen.

My belly is soft,
safe to receive,
sacred well is flowing.

My heart is open,
boundaries strong.
My power and soul now glowing.

I AM

I am Goddess.

I am golden.

I am darkness.

I am light.

I am gentle.

I am power.

I am love.

I am might.

I am all.

I am nothing.

I am particle.

I am wave.

I am rooted.

I am ready.

I am rising.

I am brave.

MEDICINE WOMAN

You are the midwife and the medicine,
the witch and the magic,
the wound and the wisdom.

You are the mess and the messenger,
the question and the answer.

Yes you.
You are it all.

Trust Your Intuition

Gaslighting your own intuition
is internalised patriarchy.
Trust yourself Witch!

Living on the Edge

The Wise and Wild Women,

living on the edge,

are those here to heal and guide our world

through the darkest times.

Weaving

From deep within,
she is remembering.
Weaving new ways
for a new world.

Sacred Daughter

We are so proud of you sacred daughter.

You carry the light so well.

Weaving our magic back home.

Our stories you will tell.

Your courage frees, heals and reveals us,

truth buried for so long.

The Great She is returning,

through you and Her sacred song.

ALL THIS RAGE

What can I do with all this rage?

Just turn the page sister.

Keep reading, keep feeling.

This is the healing.

Reclaiming.

Revealing.

Phoenix Woman

Arise now from the ashes
of the Witch Wound.
Phoenix woman.
Reclaim your power.
This is your hour.

SHE is Risen

From the tomb

of the womb

a spark is lit.

Lost wisdom coming home.

Moon and earth meet in the fleshy cave.

To birth a new we.

SHE is risen.

Part Two:

Sacred She

Mama's Home

The wise, wild, witchy power

of the Sacred Feminine

has awoken once again in the world.

Watch out.

Mama's home!

HOLY ROSE

She whispers in your blood,

Holy rose calling you home.

To yourself,

to your body,

to the sacred.

Before Patriarchy

Great Mother.

Pulse of the Earth.

Divine Feminine.

Goddess.

Before Patriarchy

SHE was as much a part of you

as your own breath.

To Remember

She has waited patiently

for thousands of years.

Giving us space to fall,

to forget,

to remember.

Always there, watching, holding, loving, trusting.

I am the dark muddy bloody cave

of the deep feminine.

I am the light.

I am the twisted roots

plunging into her damp soil.

And I am the eagle taking flight,

soaring free,

feathered and untethered.

I am both kind and a raging fire.

I am naked wild woman

and priestess in sacred robes.

Holy and whore.

Refined and raw.

Untamed and Divine.

Box me at your peril.

Game Over

Inhaling Goddess.
Exhaling patriarchy.

The Weaver

45

She is the weaver of Heaven and Earth,

spirit and matter,

human and Divine.

Magical mitochondria,

rich with codes and templates

for a new world.

Red Mary

Whore to Saint anointed.
Abuser appointed.

She needs no approval,
after millennia of removal.

Red rose She reigns.
Red rose She reigns.
Red rose She reigns.

Blood and Bone

We carry the wisdom
of those who walked this earth before,
deep in our blood and bone.
In the waves and the particles of life.
In the soil under your fingernails.
They are not gone.

Good Goddess!

48

Good Goddess!

I was starving for ritual,

parched for priestess waters,

aching for ancestral wisdom.

This drought of my soul

with empty bones,

is quenched once more.

Restored by my remembering.

Her Knowing

Beneath their lies, truth whispers.
In rest her knowing comes.
With piercing sight,
she does what's right.
Their time of rule is done.

Heed the Call

She was the Priestess,

the Wise Woman,

the Medicine Woman,

the Storyteller,

the Weaver of the red thread,

the one who knew ALL.

She is taking her place once again.

Returning.

Remembering.

Rising,

in those who heed the call.

TOGETHER WE RISE

She wears a cloak but no longer hides,
feeling the call from deep down inside.
Sounds of her soul arrive in the peace,
"Gather the women, those ripe to release".

With fire in their blood,
wounds ready to heal.
Blazing on their own terms,
a new world to reveal.

Together we birth a world of the true,
midwives and sisters, ancient and new.
Voices unheard now blast holes in the skies.

Our power returning
Together We Rise.

VENUS

Goddess of love,
union Divine,
sensual siren,
bodies entwine.

Codes of She,
creative fire,
beauty embodied,
fuel my desire.

Red Tent

Moon in my blood.
Where is my red tent?

Remembering rhythms
and cycles and lies.

That kept me forgetting
where power truly resides.

Moon in my blood
I rage and lament.
I gather my sisters
with sacred intent.

MOTHER EARTH

Wild, forgiving,

spirit living.

Rich and ancient lands.

Rivers blood.

Mountains bones.

Future in our hands.

She is us

and we are She.

Soil and soul are one.

Harming Her

we harm ourselves.

Oh, what have we done?

Wake up.

Wake up.

Wake up.

Now.

Let the healing come.

THE DRUMMERS WERE WOMEN

The drummers were women,

Frame drum of She.

Rhythm of being,

Heartbeat of We.

They drummed for the good.

They drummed for the bad.

They drummed when happy,

They drummed when sad.

They drummed for new life.

They drummed for death.

They drummed when there was nothing else left.

They drummed for the young.

They drummed for the old.

They drummed to share stories yet untold.

They drummed to feel.

They drummed to heal.

They drummed to remember, to reclaim and reveal.

Sacred Waters

She is the Source,

the river

and the estuary.

Flowing into the ocean of life.

Red Thread

Ancient sisters,
rising again.
Deep remembering
of the sacred flame.

Wounds of old,
finding peace in the now.
Holy healing,
a renewed vow.

Witch, Priestess, Wise Woman, She.
Re-woven red thread
into fabric of we.

Witch, Priestess, Wise Woman, She.
Re-woven red thread.
So mote it be.

Mother

Mother within.

Mother without.

Great Mother who unites us.

Nature Mother who provides for us.

The long-forgotten Mother Divine.

May we remember Her.

Honour Her.

Reclaim Her.

Become Her.

Fire and Flower

She is the juice,
the flow,
the form
and the formless.

She is the fire
and the flower.
Life-giver
and righteous rage.

Blood and Bone

Sacred She.

Blood and bone.

Spirit into matter.

Maiden. Mother. Crone.

Divine Feminine

To love unconditionally the real you inside,
the one you are afraid to show.

To provide shelter, nurturance and beauty.
To hear you into your Greatness and honour your truth.

To keep you safe while you adventure and risk it all.
This is her role, which comes as easily as the next breath.

The true Mother.
Divine Feminine.
Goddess.

She comes despite your defences
and cradles your trembling heart
in the palms of her hands.

The Stones

Every full moon they haunted her dreams.
Voices on a breeze: "We are the whispers in your blood".

She would wake with a longing.
A half-forgotten smoky remembering.
And then she found the stones,
Goddess in granite ring.

She could not enter in old clothes of He,
Only red robed as her sacred She.
"Welcome home my love. We have been waiting"
Embodied pledge, cells vibrating.

From each stone a priestess stepped,
Robes of light. Heart open, she wept.
Embraced and held, all memory came,
at the centre a golden flame.

Lost and found she fell to earth.
Spirit mattered, death rebirthed.

Ancient Ways

Ancient ways
from future you.
All right here
for life anew.
Reclaiming power
and voices true.
A whole new world
is coming through.

A New World

The Divine Mother appears
as one world ends.
Carrying the sacred codes
of another.

Part Three:

Making Magic

Imbolc

Fire of Imbolc, magick ablaze.
Goddess returns to herald new ways.
Seeds of tomorrow stirring on Earth.
Great Mother guide us
to remember your worth.

Rest in this womb time,
ready to rise.
For when the day comes
and scales fall from their eyes,
truth will reveal, his old ways will fall.
Your mission emerging, the Holy call.

Now weave together, standing for truth.
Trust your knowing.
No need for proof.
Your power is returning.
She burns in your veins.
Goddess reborn,
free from her chains.

Ostara

Waking Earth.
Growing light.
New beginnings,
truth ignites.

Beltane blessings from Mother Earth,
waking within the kernels of birth.
Veils are thin.
Spirit near.
Listen deep,
so you can hear.

Beltane Full Moon

Silver milk of mother moon,
fill our hearts this night,
with blooms of morrow,
new and true.

Your glow of union,
cool and clear.
Lunar Beltane,
Mystic's new year.

Sacred marriage of He and She.
Behold a new world
of Sovereign We.

Litha

Hot light of Litha,

licking my skin.

Midsummer magic,

come Holly King.

Blessings of Fae.

Rose is in bloom.

As we turn to descend

into winter womb.

72

Thank you, rich Mother,
for gifts of the land.
Harvest of hope,
held in my hands.

We gather in circle
Eating first bread.
Reep what we've sown.
We are truly blessed.

Autumn - (Mabon)

Welcome, deep in-breath of withering birth,
crunchy brown duvet hugging the earth.

As green surrenders itself to the gold,
no judgement in nature is what we've been told.

No fights for survival as gold becomes red,
no fretting about what the other leaves said.

The red does not fear the loss of its hue,
fighting to hold on to all that it knew.

Rich rainbow offers itself to the earth,
swallowed deep into the well of rebirth.

And as we each yield to the rot of the old,
we draw on the richness of gardener's gold.

Taking this food to our slumbering cave,
trusting the process of seasonal wave.

Samhain

Bowing and honouring bloodline of old.

Feminine wounds turn to wisdom foretold.

Ritual ceremony,

dance, song and fire.

Under a moon

where all dreams can transpire.

Thank you, dear ancestors,

for weaving my way,

With gifts rich and ready,

to birth a new day.

Invoking the Ancestors

Dark night I yield,

laying down my shield,

my cracked heart calls them near.

Blood line of old,

turns into gold,

rich food for my coming year.

Please guide my hand,

please help me be,

strong, grounded, loving and wise.

In these changing times,

as SHE returns,

opening sleeping eyes.

Yule

From light without,

to light within.

Darkest night,

as we begin,

the loss and shedding of old skin.

Rooted, resting, wintering.

Yule II

Shortest day,
darkest night.
Resting deep
I await the light.

New Moon

New Moon sliver,

potent scythe.

Cut ties that bind me

to wounds and lies.

Sing songs of love.

Truth and hearts aligned.

A Golden Age.

Reborn Divine.

Full Moon

Full. Ripe. Radiant.
She walks with you
into the night.
Her deep feminine pulls
upon the very cells of you.
Howl at her power.
Cast spells in her light.
Drink deep of her milky glow.
But know this.
SHE will rise anew.

Supermoon

Greatness pending, old ways ending.
Supermoon medicine, blessings sending.

Take time now to clear the way.
This moon opens a superhighway.

Release what no longer serves you best,
toxic clutter laid to rest.

Time to say NO to what feels wrong,
ready to hear your true soul song.

If it's not working. Start anew.
The months ahead will see you through.

Word and deed now aligning.
Walk the talk, integrity shining.

Dream and vision, see it clear.
Then take the steps to bring it near.

Soul Sister

Ancient soul from the future,
in the space between.
Wise and waking woman,
Priestess, Empress, Queen.

Thank you for journeying with me.
For being here right now.
Your courage and your friendship
make it easier somehow.

I honour you dear Sister.
Remember who you are.
Midwife of our tomorrows.
Beautiful blazing star.

I hope you know I love you,
and that you are not alone.
Reach out if you need to,
soul sisters to the bone.

About the Author

Kimberley Jones is a multi-award-winning Sacred Feminist, Soul Midwife and Mystical Mentor for awakening women. She is passionate about helping women unweave internalised patriarchy, reclaim their power and remember their/they're magic.

Pioneer of Healing the Witch Wound work, she is also a 4th generation Clair-everything, Channel and Medium who has worked for over 20 years with tens of thousands of women all over the world, first in clinical practice as an energy healer in a UK doctor-run Integrative Medicine Centre (where she first saw the patterns and colours of the Witch Wound in the energy fields of her clients) and then offering spiritual mentoring and readings online and by phone.

Kimberley lectured on the Witch Wound to Applied Psychology undergraduates at New York University and she is currently studying for a PhD in Ancestral Healing focussing on the Witch Wound.

Kimberley is also a professional healing artist who has exhibited internationally and is creator of 'The Witch Wound Workbook' and the free 'Healing the Witch Wound' guided meditation.
You can find more information at her website:
www.kimberleyjones.com

An Invitation

Thank you for reading Together We Rise.

Please share your feelings, feedback and photos
of the book and your favourite poems
over on social media.
#TogetherWeRise
Tag me @kimberleymjones on Instagram

Also, I'd LOVE it if you'd leave a review
on Amazon and Goodreads.

Thank you.